the **simple art** of **Japan**
origami

T0279201

the simple art of Japanese
origami

24 unique step-by-step projects

mari ono

CICO BOOKS
LONDON NEW YORK

This edition published in 2025 by CICO Books
An imprint of Ryland Peters & Small Ltd
20–21 Jockey's Fields   1452 Davis Bugg Road
London WC1R 4BW   Warrenton, NC 27589

www.rylandpeters.com

10 9 8 7 6 5 4 3 2 1

First published in 2006 as
    The Simple Art of Japanese Papercrafts

Text © Mari Ono 2006, 2025
Design, illustration, and photography ©
    CICO Books 2006, 2025

A CIP catalog record for this book is available from the
Library of Congress and the British Library.

ISBN: 978-1-80065-399-3

Printed in China

Translator: Yukiko Tagawa
Support and consulting: Chizuko Tokuno
    and Natsuko Watanabe
Editor: Robin Gurdon
Photographer: Geoff Dann
Designers: Christine Wood and Jerry Goldie
Stylist: Georgina Harris

Senior designer: Emily Breen
Art director: Sally Powell
Creative director: Leslie Harrington
Head of production: Patricia Harrington
Publishing manager: Carmel Edmonds

MIX
Paper | Supporting
responsible forestry
FSC® C106563

CONTENTS

INTRODUCTION

After the introduction of papermaking to Japan from China in the sixth century CE, papermaking underwent a rapid change in both technique and the raw materials used, so creating unique Japanese paper, or washi. Washi is thin, durable, flexible, and insect resistant, and above all, beautiful. Because of the interplay of these characteristics with the Japanese style of life, it is still used in many aspects and occasions of life in Japan. As well as being the ideal medium for writing, painting, and printing, it is used in the home to make partitions such as sliding doors and screens, lighting covers for lanterns and lamps, and fans. It is also commonly used in hobbies and amusements such as paper folding, doll making, and card games, as well as wrapping.

Among these, what attracts me most is the Japanese craft of paper folding, or origami. It needs no special tools, studio, or equipment. Everyone, from children to adults, can enjoy making almost anything with just a single piece of paper. The fun you have as you fold the creases step by step, and the surprise that you get when you have finished, is like magic. You can then go on to enjoy the variety of impressions you can create through using combinations of different colors and types of paper.

Traditionally, hats were made from shifu—fabric woven with thread twined with split washi. Now, washi can be processed into hats and dresses without the extra processes of spinning and weaving. These hats are light, durable, and waterproof.

Modern washi is used to make kyokarakami—envelopes for gifts of money—and karakami coasters. These new products have been designed by traditional washi studios in the styles of today, in the hope of spreading the use of washi through modern life.

The surfaces of this calendar have been scattered with seasonal flowers made from washi. The warm, light, hand-made touch of washi makes them especially popular.

Paper folding for amusement started sometime in Japan's Edo period (1603–1867) and has since been handed down through the generations. It once fell out of fashion but has now been revived as a figurative art, as part of the teaching materials at and schools, for rehabilitation for people of advanced years, and, of course, as amusement for everybody.

But what I like best is that you can fold your sincerity into the product you are making. It can convey your warmth whether as a gift, a gift wrapper, or as a decoration in your house. In this book, I have introduced some of the simple traditional folding designs, gift boxes, and stationery useful in our everyday life, along with guides for their creation. Included is enough paper to complete every project in this book, supplied in two sizes: 6 x 6 in (15 x 15cm) and 12 x 12 in. (30 x 30cm). To trim the papers to the required size for each project simply follow the instructions on page 18. You can also choose your own favorite papers and use them instead. I hope you enjoy making Japanese papercrafts as much as I have enjoyed making this book.

Cards decorated with origami cranes are often folded as the token of a wish or the symbol of a prayer.

Origami is now available in many beautiful color tones.

All the Japanese paper in this book can be purchased. For more details, refer to page 94.

THE HISTORY OF JAPANESE PAPERCRAFTS

Chiyo origami. Japanese chiyo origami is popular worldwide. Because of the variations of chiyo origami and because the impression of your product changes with the design of the paper, this is one of the musts in making origami or handiwork.

Papermaking was invented in China at the beginning of the second century ad and was first brought into Japan, some 400 years later, subsequent to the introduction of Buddhism in the sixth century. As part of the efforts to disseminate Buddhism, and for official use, the government encouraged paper production for the transcription of sacred sutras.

The paper first brought into Japan was weak, easy to split, and not insect resistant, making it difficult to preserve. As the demand for the production of better quality paper grew, gampi, a plant of the Daphne family indigenous to Japan was found to be an ideal raw material for paper. This prompted the Japanese to part ways with the original Chinese manufacturing method and led to the creation of Japanese paper—washi. Also, by the late eighth century, a new method of making paper from hemp and kozo (a plant of the Mulberry family), which adds the viscous mucilage of tororo-aoi (a plant of the Mallow family) was established. This is called the nagashizuki method. This development allowed the production of unusually thin, strong, and resistant paper with a minimal waste of natural resources.

At the outset of Japan's Heian period (794–1192), the regions of Japan became known for their own particular types of paper. Even today, these papers are preserved in impeccable condition in museums and private collections.

When first produced, paper was used only for official documents and the transcription of religious texts because of its scarcity and value. But increased production of quality paper soon

THE MAKING OF JAPANESE PAPER

楮たき

ちり取り

くさ打
〈打解〉

紙漉

The traditional papermaking process began with the boiling of the hemp or gampi. Excess flecks were then removed before the pulp was beaten flat. The pulp was then evenly laid out on wooden boards, and pressed, using rocks as weights. The sheets were then removed and left to dry.

おし場
〈水とり〉

紙張り

prompted it to be used for private correspondence and poetry, and hence promoted the development of literature and art. The Illustrated Handscroll Tale of Genji (1120–40) is one of such early masterpieces. The original novel, written by Murasaki Shikibu early in the eleventh century, was painted into hand scrolls.

In medieval Japan, paper was still very valuable, but it soon became useful in various parts of everyday life. Good examples of this include shoji, the paper sliding screen, and fusuma, the paper sliding door. Especially during the Edo period (1603–1867), when Japan enjoyed a time of peace, paper was used in various necessities from chochin (lanterns) and sensu (folding fans) to kamiko (robes) and even kappa (raincoats).

Folding fan. Light and durable washi makes a good fan.

The Birth of Origami

The origin of origami is not clear. It is said that one of the earliest instances of origami was decorative paperwork used in the Shinto ceremonies. Paper being a valuable commodity, it was regarded as divine and nobles would exchange letters or gifts attached with a cut paper now known as a noshi. In the samurai society, traces of origami could be seen in their special style of wrapping developed during the Muromachi period (1338–1573). But what is quite clear is that in the Edo period, when paper production increased massively, it became widely popular among ordinary townspeople. Origami cranes and various types of boat designs became popular as decorations on clothing, and are depicted in ukiyoe wood prints. The world's oldest paper-folding text book, Hiden Senbazuru Orikata (The Secret of One Thousand Origami Cranes) (1797) describes how to create many cranes connected together. This was followed by Kayaragusa (1845), which provides a comprehensive collection of origami models. Recreational origami developed as an amusement and method of decoration throughout society.

Washi Joins the World

After a long period of seclusion from the world, Japan relaxed her isolation in 1853. In 1873, at the Vienna World Exposition, Western people were surprised to see various commodities made of paper, such as parasols, rain umbrellas, folding fans, and fabrics made from shifu, which were exhibited by Japan. For Westerners, paper was merely a medium of writing, painting, and printing. Washi's thin and soft but resilient characteristics enabled the Japanese to use it in various ways from daily necessities to recreational and artistic use. Washi is now actively used in various categories of work: arts, crafts, bookbinding, graphic design, and interior design to name a few. Origami is not only a popular amusement among children but it has become a hobby for adults. It is used for recreational purposes, but there are now many origami creators whose works have even reached the level of fine art.

Washi letter set. Unryushi has thick dominant fibers on the surface, which gives a deep impression on those who receive the letter. This is a perfect material to convey your sincere heart.

TYPES OF JAPANESE PAPER — **WASHI**

Included with this book is a selection of papers to get you started, but Japan has a rich history of beautiful, ornate papers that you can use instead. There are many types of traditional Japanese papers available, known in their native country as washi, which are easy to use for paper folding (*origami*) or paper crafts, but each type's suitability depends on its characteristics and composition. The following pages give a brief explanation of some of the different papers available.

The Chinese character representing the word for "paper" can be read in three ways in Japanese: kami, gami, or shi. The use of each form depends on the sentence and surrounding words: kami is used only on its own, and simply means "paper." Gami and shi mean the same thing but are both used as descriptions when attached to other words. Which one is used depends on the form of the word to which it is joined.

PLAIN PAPERS

Danshi, or Ceremony Paper, and **Taireishi**

Danshi is a thick, elegant white paper with a furrowed or creped texture, and is made from the fibers of the kozo, or mulberry tree. It was originally used for formal letters and diplomas, especially in the Heian period (794–1192), when court ladies favored it for writing poems. It is now used to wrap gifts and for making envelopes to hold a gift of money at weddings and other special occasions, including New Year. Taireishi has short fibers of mulberry visible on the surface of the paper and is used to print formal letters and documents. It is made at Echizen, in the present day Fukui prefecture, which is especially famous for production of washi.

Momigami

Momigami is a Japanese washi paper that has been scrunched up. It is often used for doll-making and mounting paintings or calligraphy because it is thin but strong. It is also suitable for gift wrapping and origami. The image on this page is a variation of momigami called habutaeshi. The paper has both sides printed with different colors and designs to make a fashionable gift-wrapping paper.

Tengujoshi, Rakusuishi, and Unryushi

Each of these papers is extremely thin, made using the most sophisticated techniques. Tengujoshi was described as "thin as a mayfly's wing" but is nonetheless extremely strong. It was originally used for artists' tracing paper, block copy for woodblock prints, and backing paper. Currently, it is used for wrapping jewelry and pieces of fine art as well as for restoring cultural properties. The image also shows the thin papers known as rakusuishi and unryushi. Light filtering through these beautiful thin papers produces warmth and soft beauty. They are used for shoji, the translucent sliding screen and chochin, the Japanese lantern. Enjoy the delicate silky touch of these papers in wrapping.

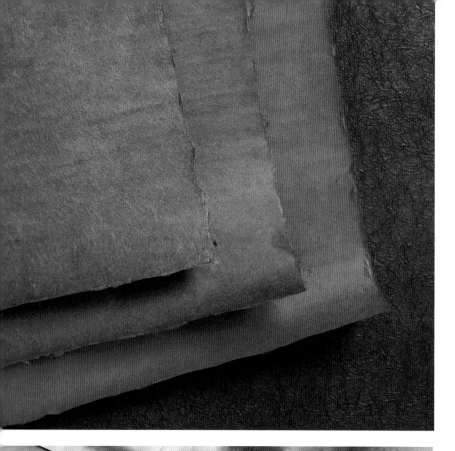

Mingeishi

Mingeishi is a general term for handmade washi which were produced from the 1920s in various parts of Japan as a result of the Mingei (folk craft) movement lead by the philosopher, Muneyoshi Yanagi who especially appreciated the beauty of everyday items created by nameless artisans. Some of the gampishi, the traditional handmade paper dating back to ancient times, is also produced as a type of mingeishi. Most of the mingeishi are kozo papers made from mulberry which makes them strong and resistant to tearing. They are still used widely for daily items such as envelopes, fusuma (sliding doors) and book binding.

Itajimezomeshi

During the Edo period (1603–1867), people started making paper flowers for decoration at temples. To make them look more realistic, a paper dyeing method called itajimezome was invented. Two pieces of wood (ita) are wrapped with folded (jime) plain paper. They are clamped together, before part of the paper is dyed (zome), creating a pattern which repeats itself when the paper is unfolded. The design can differ according to the way the paper is folded. It is popular now for origami and gift-wrapping.

PATTERNED PAPERS

Kyo chiyogami

Chiyogami is a decorative paper that is either printed using woodblocks or, alternatively, colored in a method similar to that used for dyeing kimonos; the name Kyo refers to the region of Kyoto in which the paper is made. The designs are taken from various court nobles' patterns and kimono, or yuzen, patterns. Shown here are the traditional and chic small patterns of kyo chiyogami which are also suitable for origami.

Kyo karakami

Karakami is made by printing designs with a woodblock stamp onto already beautifully dyed paper. The name originally referred to all the decorative papers imported from China in the Heian period (794–1192) that were used for painting and calligraphy. But they were soon imitated and produced in Japan. By the Muromachi period (1338–1573), strong and durable, yet decorative, karakami came to be used as fusuma (sliding doors) and tsuitate (screens), which were indispensable as partitions in houses built at that time. The paper shown here is made at the Karacho studio which was established during the Edo period. It is still used for fusuma at the Imperial Palaces as well as in high-grade interior decoration.

Edo chiyogami

Edo chiyogami is made in the Tokyo region and differs stylistically from kyo chiyogami by being more brightly colored and fashionable. Chiyogami originated in Kyoto, but when it was brought to Edo during the period in which Tokyo dominated the country it became linked with the woodblock printing technique of ukiyoe, and chiyogami with popular designs such as kabuki and sumo was produced. Nowadays, the paper is used as a material for handicrafts and various everyday items as well as interior decoration and stationery.

Sarasagami and katazomeshi

This is a stencil-dyed paper using patterns brought into Japan through trade with Spain and Portugal in the sixteenth century. Using washi laminated with persimmon tannin as the stencils, an Indonesian or other ethnic pattern is printed on the paper. It is used for handicrafts as well as fusuma and shoji in houses.

THE BASIC TECHNIQUES FOR **ORIGAMI**

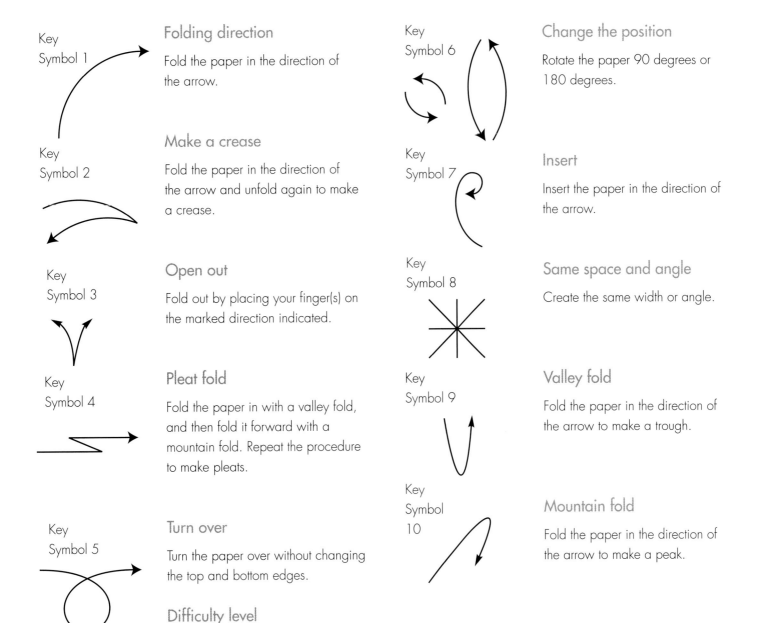

Key Symbol 1

Folding direction

Fold the paper in the direction of the arrow.

Key Symbol 2

Make a crease

Fold the paper in the direction of the arrow and unfold again to make a crease.

Key Symbol 3

Open out

Fold out by placing your finger(s) on the marked direction indicated.

Key Symbol 4

Pleat fold

Fold the paper in with a valley fold, and then fold it forward with a mountain fold. Repeat the procedure to make pleats.

Key Symbol 5

Turn over

Turn the paper over without changing the top and bottom edges.

Key Symbol 6

Change the position

Rotate the paper 90 degrees or 180 degrees.

Key Symbol 7

Insert

Insert the paper in the direction of the arrow.

Key Symbol 8

Same space and angle

Create the same width or angle.

Key Symbol 9

Valley fold

Fold the paper in the direction of the arrow to make a trough.

Key Symbol 10

Mountain fold

Fold the paper in the direction of the arrow to make a peak.

Difficulty level

The complexity of each project in the book has been calculated on a scale of 1–5. Level 1 is the simplest, while level 5 requires the use of some complex folding techniques. If you allow yourself to gain confidence gradually you will soon be successfully creating the most intricate of designs.

BASIC FOLDING TECHNIQUES

Square Fold

1 Fold a piece of square paper in half to make a triangle.

2 Fold it in half again.

3 Lift and open the top triangular pocket, refolding it to make a square.

4 Turn the paper over and lift up the remaining triangular point.

5 Again, open out the fold and flatten it, to make a square.

Triangle Fold

1 Fold a piece of square paper in half to make a rectangle.

2 Fold it in half again to make a square.

3 Open out the top square pocket, refolding it to make a triangle.

4 Turn the paper over and lift the other square to the vertical.

5 Open out the square, reshaping it to make a triangle as in step 3.

BASIC **ZABUTON**, OR FLOOR CUSHION SHAPE

1 Mark the center of a square piece of paper by lightly folding in half from corner to corner. Fold the first corner into the center.

2 Turn the paper through 90 degrees and fold the next corner into the center.

3 When all four corners have been folded in, the zabuton is complete.

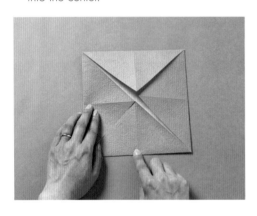

A TIP FOR CUTTING PAPER

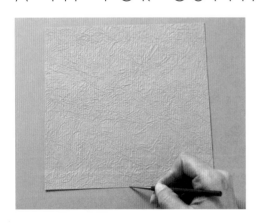

1 Mark the start and end points of your intended cut with an awl.

2 Set the metal edge of the ruler on the points marked in step 1. Cut along the ruler using the paper cutter. Be certain that the tip of the cutter follows the edge of the ruler.

A TIP FOR FOLDING THICK PAPER

1 Mark the starting and end points of your intended mountain fold with an awl. If you want to make a valley fold, make the crease for your intended fold on the reverse side of the paper.

2 Set the ruler on the points marked in step 1 and draw a line along the ruler using the awl, without cutting the paper. Make a mountain fold along the line you have just drawn.

INSIDE FOLD

1 Following the dotted line in the diagram, make a crease at the tip of the triangle.

2 Unfold.

3 Open out the paper and fold the tip along the crease to make a mountain fold.

4 Make a valley fold between the mountain folds.

5 Fold the valley fold inside.

THE PROJECTS

ORIZURU—
CRANE

This the origami crane is perhaps the most famous design among the traditional Japanese paper-folding models. It is also one of the most tricky, but once you learn how to fold the crane, you should be able to make any design in this book. The crane has been regarded as a symbol of longevity in Japan since ancient times. You can make a nice greeting card (see pages 68–69) by applying it as an accent, or use lovely paper to make it a gift in itself.

MATERIALS

◆ **1 sheet of patterned paper, 6 x 6 in. (15 x 15cm)**

Difficulty level: 3

1 Begin with a square fold (see page 16). Fold the paper in half diagonally, then in half again to make a triangle.

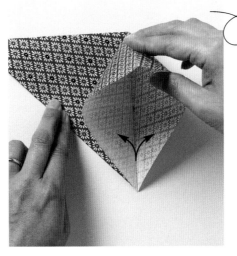

2 Open the upper pocket to make a square and flatten.

3 Turn the object over, and open out the pocket to make a square.

4 Fold the left and right flaps of the top layer into the center so that they meet in the middle.

5 Turn the object over, and repeat the previous step with the back flaps.

6 Fold the top triangle down to make a marker crease along the top of the tolded flaps, and release.

7 Open the outer flaps and use the marker crease from the previous step to lift the top layer of paper toward the top.

8 Push the far tip right of the diamond out so that the colored edges meet in the middle.

9 Turn the object over and repeat the previous two steps on the reverse so that you are left with a tall diamond-shaped object.

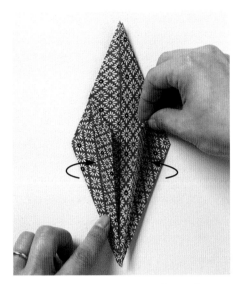

10 Fold the outer edges of both flaps on the top layer inward to meet at the center. Turn over and repeat with the reverse side.

11 Make marker creases at the top of both of the object's arms, and release.

12 Open out the flap and make a reverse fold along one of the crease lines you have just made.

13 Close the flap around the folded up arm. Repeat the previous two steps on the other side.

14 Make a slanted fold halfway up one arm, unfold and fold it inside along the crease to make an inside fold for the crane's head.

15 Pull the wings downward and gently expand the crane's back to finish.

KUSU DAMA—
DECORATIVE SPHERES

Inspired by Japanese kusu dama—hanging charms used to ward off sickness and evil spirits—these balls combine contrasting sheets of colored paper to create fun, decorative gifts. They have many possible uses: insert a bag of pot-pourri before you close up the ball to act as an air freshener, or enclose a bell to make a traditional Japanese baby's toy that will ring as a toddler rolls it about. Alternatively, to westernize the decoration, make the ball from shiny paper and hang it from a bouquet of flowers or a Christmas tree.

MATERIALS
- ◆ **6 sheets of patterned paper, 6 x 6 in. (15 x 15cm)**
- ◆ **Paper glue**
- ◆ **Cocktail stick**

Difficulty level: 2

1 Take one piece of paper and fold it in half, making a diagonal crease from corner to corner. Open up and make a fold between the other two corners.

2 Fold one corner after another into the center, until you end up with another square shape.

3 Finish the square by folding in the final corner.

4 Turn over the paper and fold all the corners into the center.

5 Once again, turn the paper over and fold all the corners into the center.

6 Place a fingertip under one of the flaps at each corner and pull it open, creating a squared off arm at all four corners.

7 Repeat this whole process with five other sheets of paper. Begin joining them together by slotting one arm inside another.

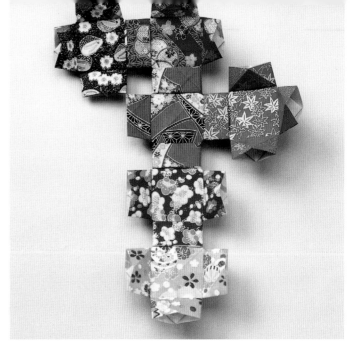

8 To fix the pieces in place, use a cocktail stick to insert a little paper glue between the sheets at every joint.

9 Connect all the pieces of paper together until they lie flat in the shape shown above. If necessary, you can make a slight crease on the arm being inserted to help the fit.

12 Check that each join is equal, making an even sphere.

11 Complete the final link, finishing the ball, remembering to insert a bell or bag of pot-pourri now if you choose.

10 Turn over and begin slotting the remaining arms together, gluing each join in place with paper glue.

IRO BAKO—COLOR CUBE

Just as with the kusu dama (see pages 26–9), the color cube is created by combining six pieces of origami folded in the same way. You can make a cube by mixing and matching colors and designs in any way you like—you can even make color cubes of different sizes. One of the most traditional methods of folding origami, the cube can be given to children as a toy, or used as a room decoration. Alternatively, put some candy in it and use it as goodie bag at a children's party, or it could be a box that contains a mystery gift.

MATERIALS
- ◆ **6 sheets of plain paper, 6 x 6 in. (15 x 15cm)**

Difficulty level: 2

1 Take one sheet and fold in half to create the valley fold and unfold. Fold the top and bottom edges to the center. In this way, you have four vertical creases.

2 Unfold it again. Make a valley fold in the top left hand corner by folding the tip down to the nearest valley fold, then turn the paper round and repeat in what was the bottom right corner.

3 Fold the top and bottom edges in to the center fold.

4 Fold the bottom left corner up to the top edge and then hold it in place by slipping it under the top flap.

5 Turn the paper round and fold down the same corner before also putting it under the flap.

6 Turn it over, and fold both ends into the center to make a square. Release the points to leave two marker creases. The first piece is now complete.

7 Repeat steps 1 to 6 until you have made six pieces. Slot four of the pieces around the first by fitting the ends into the openings together in the pattern shown. Turn the combined papers over and lift the pieces up, slotting them together to make the sides of the box.

8 Fit the last piece in on the top as a lid, and fix it by guiding the box's two remaining ends into position.

TSUNOKOBAKO—
DECORATION BOX

This traditional origami design for holding sweets or trinkets is so simple that even a small child could make it. Like many of the most enduring origami designs, it has been handed down from mother to child. Here, the enchanting floral design is combined with plain paper. Alternatively, you can make it with any size of paper or with a single piece of paper if you prefer.

MATERIALS

- ◆ **1 sheet of plain paper, 6 x 6 in. (15 x 15cm)**
- ◆ **1 sheet of patterned paper, 6 x 6 in. (15 x 15cm)**
- ◆ **Paper glue**
- ◆ **Cocktail stick**

Difficulty level: 2

1 Glue two sheets of paper together. Begin with a square fold then fold both sides back to the center. Turn over and repeat.

2 Rotate through 180 degrees and open out the pocket.

3 Fold the flaps in the direction of the arrows to make valley folds.

4 Turn over and repeat step 3.

5 Fold the outer half of the flaps you made in steps 3 and 4 to the center to make mountain folds.

6 Turn over and do the same with the reverse side.

7 Turn down the center flap before repeating on the other side.

8 Fold the four upper tips down.

9 Open to a box shape by pushing up on the bottom.

10 You can make pleat folds with the tips if you like.

FUSEN — BALLOON

Handed down from mother to child, there are many traditional origami models which are still being folded today. One of the oldest among them is this balloon. A single sheet of paper folds flat before being inflated with a single breath to become a three-dimensional toy ball. This balloon will teach you the pleasure of origami folding—it is simple to make and you can increase your enjoyment of making it with different sizes and colors of paper. This is one of the magical origami models, dating from the days when there were not many toys for children to play with.

MATERIALS

♦ **1 sheet of patterned paper, 6 x 6 in. (15 x 15cm)**

Difficulty level: 2

1 Begin to create a triangle fold (see page 17) by making a pair of cross-shaped creases with valley folds.

2 Fold the paper in half, again with a valley fold.

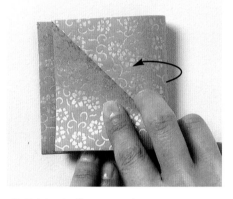

3 Fold in half again to form a square with a valley fold.

4 Open the upper pocket out into a triangle.

5 Turn over and lift the upper flap to the vertical.

6 Press down, opening the pocket out into a triangle.

7 Fold the corners of the upper flap to meet the triangle's apex.

8 Turn over and repeat, folding the two corners to the apex to make a square.

9 Fold the right and left corners to the center with a valley fold.

10 Turn over and repeat the previous step.

11 Fold the upper tips of the top layer down toward the center to split a triangle in half, and repeat on the other side.

12 Fold the triangular shaped flap you just made and tuck it into the top pocket. Repeat this for the other side of the top layer, and for the reverse side.

13 Fold down the far tip and score the fold before releasing. Repeat on the reverse side.

14 Open the flaps out into a cross shape and blow gently through the hole, slowly inflating the balloon while easing out the creases.

KABUTO—SAMURAI HELMET

Every year in May the Japanese mark Children's Day. One of the ways of celebrating the healthy growth and development of boys is by decorating kabuto, or samurai helmets, a traditional origami design. For a larger version that a child can wear, we often make this kabuto with a sheet of newspaper. It is a great project for a child to make with as it is very simple and they will love wearing it

MATERIAL

◆ **1 sheet of patterned paper,
6 x 6 in. (15 x 15cm)**

Difficulty level: 1

1 Fold in half, and then fold both corners of the triangle to meet at the bottom tip, creating a square.

2 Rotate the paper through 180 degrees and fold up the right and left flaps in half to meet at the top of the object.

3 Fold the top flaps away from the vertical center line, creating triangles.

4 Fold the upper flap of the bottom half away from you, leaving its tip about ⅝ in. (1.5cm) below the object's upper tip.

5 Fold the bottom of the flap made in step 4 away from you, using the center line as the crease line.

6 Turn and slide the bottom flap up inside the helmet to finish. Mount the hat on a stand or stick it to card to make an artwork.

TATO BAKO — CAKE BOX

Perhaps the most important tip for creating a perfect gift box is to make neat and accurate creases. This box might seem a little complicated, but it needs extra care only in the last steps when assembling the box. You can make a box of any size depending on the size of the paper you have. Here, I used modern paper with a cosmic design but you can have fun changing the design of paper to suit the occasion.

MATERIALS

◆ **1 sheet of patterned paper, 12 x 12 in. (30 x 30cm)**

Difficulty level: 5

1 Make a cross-shaped crease, and fold each corner into the center to make the zabuton or floor cushion (see page 18).

2 Unfold, and fold the top and bottom edges to the center to make valley folds. Unfold, rotate the paper 90 degrees and repeat.

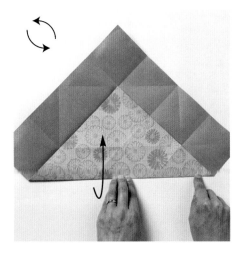

3 Rotate the paper 45 degrees and bring the bottom corner up toward the top point, folding it in line with the outer set of creases. Repeat at all four corners.

4 Make short valley folds across the squares nearest each corner. Make a sharp crease.

5 Fold the sheet over, placing the same marks together and make the creases across each corner.

6 When all the creases across the corners have been made the sheet should look like this.

7 Turn the paper over again, and pinch together the crease at the top right.

8 Begin to stand the right edge up by turning the pinched edge up on itself.

9 Pinch the mountain fold at the adjacent corner and put the left flap over the right flap to create the first corner of the box.

10 While holding the corner with your right hand so as not to allow it to reopen, repeat the previous step to make the left corner.

11 When you are finished with the second corner, hold both corners and proceed with the third corner.

12 While keeping the top of the box together, fold the last corner and prepare to slot it into the top.

13 Finish by arranging the top of the box to look neat.

AYAME—IRIS

The traditional paper-folding design of the iris flower creates a solid and romantic piece. The secret of making a perfect iris is to ensure each corner is folded sharply, and to make sure the paper edges fit together neatly and tightly to within a hair's breadth. The final step of adding a curl on the petals is a lovely finishing touch. It may seem difficult at the beginning, but as there are many repetitive steps in folding the iris, you will find success after practicing a few times. Here I have made a series of iris flowers and put them in a glass vase—enjoy arranging them in your own original way.

MATERIALS

◆ **1 sheet of plain paper,
   6 x 6 in. (15 x 15cm)**

◆ **A pencil or round stick**

Difficulty level: 5

1 Begin by making a square fold (see page 16). Fold one pocket over to make a crease. Unfold and open up the pocket and refold along the crease you just made.

2 Turn over and repeat on the other pockets to make a square.

3 Fold the left hand flap across the center and fold forward.

4 Turn the object over and repeat on the other side.

5 Fold one side of the small triangle into the middle.

6 Open out the other flaps and repeat the previous step.

7 Rotate the object 180 degrees so that the divided flaps point away from you. Now fold the points back to meet at the bottom in the center, repeating this procedure on every flap.

8 Open these folds out and use them as marker folds, pushing down the lower part of the fold so that the paper meets along the vertical. Repeat on every flap.

9 Fold up the bottom triangle of each of the four sections.

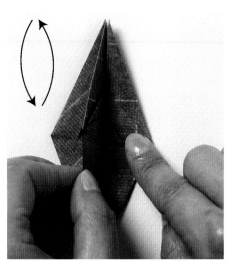

10 Turn the object back through 180 degrees and fold each flap in half.

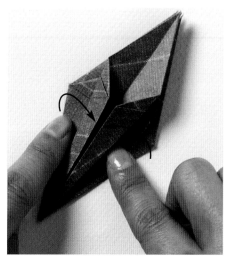

11 Fold the outer edges of the top flap in to meet in the center. Repeat on the other flaps.

12 To open out the petals, fold down one end of each flap which was folded in the previous step.

13 When all four are bent over, curl down the tips of every flap with a pencil.

MONKIRIASOBI—PAPERCUTTING

Monkiriasobi combines the skills of origami and paper cutting. After folding, surprisingly beautiful designs can be made from cutting patterns into square paper. Monkiriasobi became widespread in Japan during the Edo period (1603–1867) when popular culture flourished. In particular, family crests called kamon and snow crystals were popular designs in those days.

You can use your papercut pieces on accessories, coasters, and ornaments in your room.

MATERIALS

◆ **1 sheet of plain paper, 6 x 6 in. (15 x 15cm)**

◆ **Protractor**

◆ **Pencil**

◆ **Scissors**

Difficulty level: 2

1 Fold the paper in half to make a triangle, and use the protractor to fold the right corner up toward the top at an angle of 36 degrees.

2 Fold the right side again at the same angle, and fold the left corner along the crease you just made with the right corner.

3 Fold the left corner along the right edge to make a valley fold. At this stage ensure that the edges of the object align.

4 Lightly draw in the pattern you will cut with a pencil.

5 Cut along the lines of the design with scissors.

6 Open up the paper carefully, so as not to tear it.

SUIREN—WATER LILY

The water lily, or lotus flower, has long been beloved as the pure and sacred flower of Buddha. Although the traditional design of the water lily is simple, the finished flower is very pretty. Once you have learnt how to fold it, you can make it for your friends and family. You can arrange them on a flat plate or use the lotus leaf as a bowl for candy with which to entertain your guests.

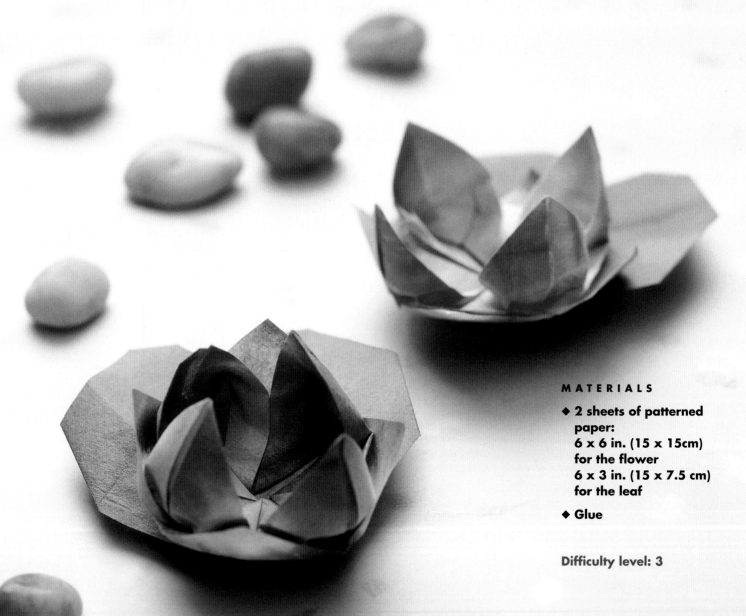

MATERIALS
- ◆ **2 sheets of patterned paper:**
  **6 x 6 in. (15 x 15cm)
  for the flower
  6 x 3 in. (15 x 7.5 cm)
  for the leaf**

- ◆ **Glue**

Difficulty level: 3

LOTUS FLOWER

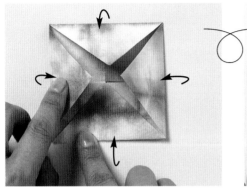

1 Begin by making the basic zabuton, or floor cushion shape (see page 18), and repeat.

2 Turn over and again fold the four corners into the center.

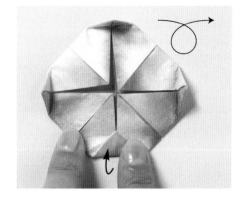

3 Fold in the tips of the four edges about ½ in. (10mm) to make valley folds.

4 Turn over. While holding the tips made in step 3, bring the tips of four flaps in the center to the reverse side.

5 Gently bring the four flaps to the reverse side and make them round with your finger.

6 Smooth out the base of the flower by pulling the tips while holding the flower.

LOTUS LEAF

1 Make a horizontal crease in the middle of the paper.

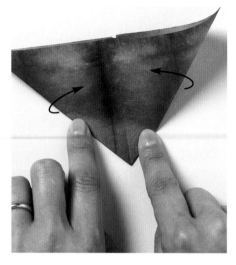

2 Fold both edges under to meet in the center on the reverse side.

3 Fold the right side of the triangle up to meet the center crease and open up the reverse side. Repeat the same procedure for the left side.

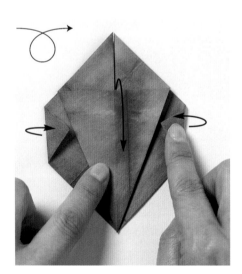

4 Turn over. Fold right and left corners in. Open the middle pocket to the center crease and fold it down as in the previous step.

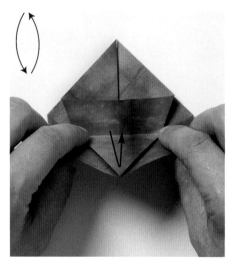

5 Spin the object through 180 degrees, then fold down the two tips from the top to make creases. Unfold.

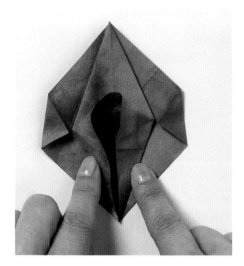

6 Fold the tips inward.

7 Turn over and fold back tips at the top away from the center.

8 Fold back the new topmost points.

9 Turn the leaf over and paste the lotus flower onto it at the pointed end of the leaf with a dab of glue.

HAKO — SQUARE BOX

It is simple to create a gift box from just a single sheet of paper with origami techniques that use neither scissors nor glue. Any paper will do, as long as you can divide it into two squares of similar, but not identical, size—from these you can make a gorgeous box with a lid. You can make any size of box; and even make boxes of different sizes and pile them into one another, one by one.

MATERIALS

◆ 2 sheets of patterned paper: one for lid and one for box, depending on size of box required (see table opposite for sizing)

Difficulty level: 2

Paper size for lid	6 x 6 in. 15 x 15cm	8 x 8 in. 20 x 20cm	10 x 10 in. 25 x 25cm	12 x 12 in. 30 x 30cm
Size of lid	2¼ x 2¼ x 1 in. 5.5 x 5.5 x 2.5cm	3 x 3 x 1½ in. 7.5 x 7.5 x 3.5cm	3½ x 3½ x 1¾ in. 8.5 x 8.5 x 4.5cm	4½ x 4½ x 2¼ in. 10.5 x 10.5 x 5.5cm
Paper size for box	5½ x 5½ in. 14 x 14cm	7½ x 7½ in. 19 x 19cm	9 x 9 in. 24 x 24cm	11¼ x 11¼ in. 28.5 x 28.5cm
Size of box	2 x 2 x ⅞ in. 5 x 5 x 2.4cm	2½ x 2½ x 1⅜ in. 6.5 x 6.5 x 3.4cm	3¼ x 3¼ x 1⅜ in. 8 x 8 x 4.4cm	4 x 4 x 2⅜ in. 10 x 10 x 5.4cm

1 Make a cross-shaped crease, and fold each corner to the center to make the basic zabuton or floor cushion (see page 18). Precision at this stage will be helpful later.

2 Fold the top and bottom edges to the center to make valley folds before unfolding again to the shape of a zabuton.

3 Turn the paper through 90 degrees and make valley folds as in step 2 before again unfolding to a zabuton shape and opening out the top and bottom flaps as in the photo.

4 Taking two neighboring edges, make two sides of the box by lifting them toward the vertical. Ensure that the fold creating the corner of the box is inside the box. Fold the top flap back inside over the crease to make the corner of the box.

5 Repeat step 4 for the crease on the other side.

6 Fold the flap inside.

7 Repeat the whole process on the opposite side.

For the lid: refer to the table above for the paper sizes and make another box in exactly the same way but with slightly larger dimensions as described.

NAGA BAKO—RECTANGLE BOX

Just as you created a square box (see pages 54–5), here we will create a rectangular gift box. A box made with an elegant gift wrap paper that you have to hand can add a unique touch to an ordinary gift. Anyone who receives a gift in this handmade box may appreciate it even more. This box can be used not only as a gift box but also for keeping handy items, like your spectacles, on the desk at home. If the box is to contain heavy items, apply cardboard to the bottom and four sides when folding the paper.

MATERIALS

◆ 2 sheets of patterned paper:
   11 x 11 in. (28 x 28cm) for
   the box
   12 x 12 in. (30 x 30cm) for
   the lid

Difficulty level: 2

1 Fold the sheet in half diagonally. Mark the point ⅓ of the way from the tip to the fold line and make a crease.

2 Open out the paper. Fold top and bottom creases made in step 1 to make valley folds and then fold both sides into the center.

3 Fold the top and bottom flaps toward the center, making valley folds.

4 Fold in the right and left sides to make valley folds.

5 Fold the top and bottom sides into the center and unfold.

6 Turn the paper through 90 degrees and fold the top and bottom sides to make creases before unfolding the top and bottom corners.

7 Fold the left horizontal crease to stand the left side upright and then fold the top flap inside to make the corner of the box. Repeat the step on the right side.

8 Fold the flap inside and do the same with the opposite side.

HASHI BUKURO—
CHOPSTICKS WRAPPER

Wrapping chopsticks in paper can add an Asian flair to your oriental-style home party. Chopstick wrappers were originally made by Japanese chefs to accompany the meal. In the home, chopstick wrappers were, and still are, used on special occasions, such as New Year's Day, and decorated with paper cut-outs or the names of family members. To finish your table setting, put the chopsticks inside the wrapper.

MATERIALS

◆ **1 sheet of paper, 7 x 12 in. (18 x 30cm)**
◆ **Paper decorations cut in the shape of cherry flowers and maple leaves**
◆ **Glue**
◆ **Cocktail Stick**

Difficulty level: 1

1 Fold the paper in half and then each half again into the center to make marker creases. Unfold and turn the top left corner down to the center crease.

2 Start folding from the bottom up into the center, making valley folds, and continue until the object is the width of one fold.

3 Turn over the end, marking the crease when the turned end is level with the visible edge of the turned corner.

4 Fold back the plain end, turning it at right angles and making a mountain fold.

5 Lift the paper and wrap the tail end once around the bottom of the object.

6 Fold the end of the tail into a triangle along the side of the object before turning the end over and tucking it in place.

7 Cut out a cherry leaf or maple flower shape, using the templates below as a guide if necessary. Fold the flower or leaf around the edge of the wrapper and fix it in place with a glue-covered cocktail stick.

KINPU—MONEY WRAPPER

Japan has a custom of giving gifts of money on special occasions to convey feelings of congratulation, gratitude, or even condolence. The folded envelope used to wrap these gifts of money is called the kinpu. It can be made from various designs, but the most important thing when you are making your envelope is to choose a pattern that will convey your feelings. The envelope can also also be used to cover cards, photographs, or paintings, and you might choose to finish the project with ribbons or paper string.

MATERIALS

- ◆ **1 sheet of patterned paper, 12 x 12 in. (30 x 30cm)**
- ◆ **1 sheet of white paper, 11½ x 11½ in. (29 x 29cm)**
- ◆ **Glue**
- ◆ **Ribbon, optional**

Difficulty level: 3

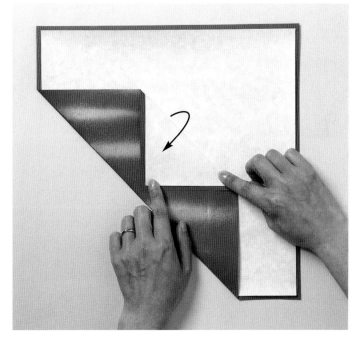

1 Paste the white paper onto the reverse side of the patterned paper with a small amount of glue at the four corners. Fold the bottom left corner three-quarters of the way toward its opposite, making a valley fold.

2 Fold the tip of the flap to meet the left edge of the object, making a pleat fold.

3 Fold the right flap over toward the left, using the pleat fold as the fold line.

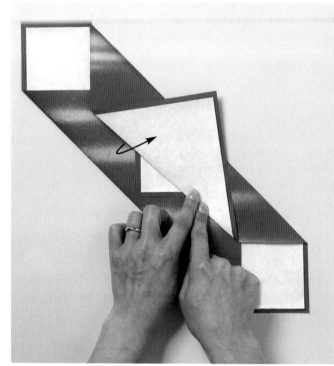

4 Fold the tip of the right flap back along the center line to make a mountain fold.

5 While leaving ½ in. (1 cm) for the tip, fold the right flap back on itself to make a pleat fold.

6 After placing the money or gift inside, fold the ends underneath the object.

7 Place money inside the envelope and, for an authentic touch tie a ribbon around the outside.

POCHIBUKURO—
MONEY-GIFT ENVELOPE

In Japan, it was once considered rude to give money unwrapped so this small envelope is used to hold coins or folded bills with which to show one's gratitude. As the pochibukuro is now also used to hold money given on special occasions I have made a small version which could contain coins, stamps, and small gifts. As the back of the paper also appears in the front, you could try two different types of paper pasted together—you can develop your own individual designs.

MATERIAL

◆ 1 sheet of patterned paper, 6 x 6 in. (15 x 15cm)

Difficulty level: 2

1 Make a pair of cross-shaped marker creases. Unfold and find the distance one-third of the way along one crease. Fold the tip over along this line and score the fold.

2 Fold the previously turned tip back to the outside of the piece.

3 Fold the tip back in half once more, ensuring that it is not folded over the center line.

4 Turn the right hand tip over so that it touches the top left edge of the turned bottom tip.

5 Repeat steps 2 and 3 for the left flap.

6 Turn the top tip down to the outer edge of the object and repeat steps 2 and 3 once more.

7 Turn the left hand tip over to the far side of the piece, creating a square.

8 Repeat steps 2 and 3 again then lift up and open the bottom so that the left hand side can be tucked in.

9 Flatten and tuck in the flaps so that the final envelope is perfectly symmetrical.

ORIGAMI CARD—GREETINGS CARD

If you make this greetings card with colorful paper, it will be perfect to give for a birthday or with a congratulatory gift. The crane is auspicious in Japan and is a symbol of longevity. One thousand origami cranes are frequently sent to the sick to pray for recovery from illness and for long life. So, I suggest using the crane to decorate congratulations cards as well as get-well cards. Your original handmade card adds heartfelt love to the words inside.

MATERIALS/FAN

- **8½ x 6 in. (A5/21 x 15cm) card stock**
- **Patterned paper (A) for fan, 6 x 3 in. (15 x 7.5cm)**
- **Plain paper (B) for lining 6 x 6 in. (15 x 15cm)**
- **Ribbon, optional**
- **Paper cutter**
- **Ruler**
- **Glue**
- **Pencil**

Difficulty level: 3

1 To make the fan, fold in paper A ¼ in. (5mm) from both edges, and make pleat folds of ⅜ in. (1cm) width, creating an appearance like a concertina.

2 Fold paper B in half, and paste it on the card stock making the center of the paper and card stock meet each other. Apply the glue sparingly in spots as needed—too much glue may make the paper wrinkle.

3 Apply glue on both edges of the fan made in step 1, and paste it onto the center of paper B.

4 If you wish, attach a ribbon to each side of the fan to add extra decorative detail.

MATERIALS/CRANES

- **8½ x 6 in. (A5/21 x 15cm) card stock**
- **Paper cutter**
- **2 sheets of patterned paper, 6 x 6 in. (15 x 15cm) and 2½ x 2½ in. (6 x 6cm)**
- **1 sheet of colored paper, 6 x 6 in. (15 x 15cm), cut into 1½ x 1½ in. (3.5 x 3.5cm) diamonds**
- **Ruler**
- **Glue**

Difficulty level: 3

1 Paste the three small colored diamond shapes onto the center of the front of the card stock.

2 Make a pair of cranes, one small and one large. (see pages 22–25). Paste one side of the wing of the large crane inside the card to the right of the center fold and cut around the outline of the wing so as to form a triangle when opened.

3 Paste one side of the wing of the small crane to the front of the card and repeat on the other side for the large crane.

HANA BAKO—FLOWER BOX

This simply folded box is ideal as a gift box for flowers to be given away at a wedding. It can also be used either as a flower vase or a flower pot if you line it with thick card and place silver foil inside as waterproofing. Continue the floral theme by making the box from paper decorated with leaves and flowers. You could even try making a matching greetings card or gift box to go with your flowers.

MATERIALS
- ◆ **1 sheet of patterned paper, 12 x 12 in. (30 x 30cm)**
- ◆ **Glue**

Difficulty level: 1

1 Make mountain folds from corner to corner, then open out and repeat on the other diagonal. Open the sheet out again and half it with valley folds top-to-bottom, and side-to-side.

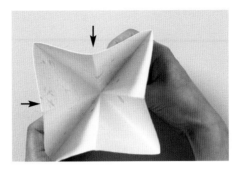

2 Pick up the paper and squeeze it together into the square.

3 Mark a point ¾ in. (2cm) from the bottom, fold the tip up, and score.

4 Mark 1½ in. (3.5cm) from the far tip and fold the upper flap forward, then turn the object over and repeat.

5 Fold both upper flaps together so that their tips meet in the center. Turn over and repeat on the object's other side.

6 Paste the flaps to both sides of box and unfold.

7 Raise the folded flaps and open the box by prising it open from the inside. Fold four corners at the top to make mountain folds.

8 Gently flatten out the bottom of the box to give the box its final shape.

KAZARIZURU—FANTAIL CRANE

At New Year in Japan, houses and rooms are prepared with special decorations. Like Christmas in the West, families come together, and celebrate the festival with special food. I made this fantail crane as a New Year's decoration. If you fold it using patterned paper of European design, you can create a pretty ornament. If you fold it with a small sheet of paper, for a chopstick rest, then it will be a suitable decoration for a party table. It may look difficult at first, but the simple repetition of the folding will just enhance your enjoyment of paper folding. Make sure your creases are accurate in order to give an elegant finish.

MATERIALS

◆ **1 sheet of plain paper 12 x 12 in. (30 x 30cm)**

Difficulty level: 5

1 Begin with the square fold (see page 16) and then fold the front flaps to meet in the center.

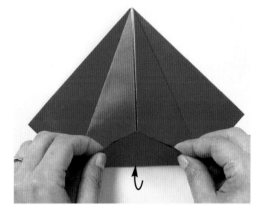

2 Fold the bottom triangle up to make a crease.

3 Unfold all three scored creases. Raise, open, and flatten the front flaps.

4 Turn the object over onto its back. Fold the right flap over, to cover the left.

5 Open up the flap you just folded to the left, and flatten it. Open up the left flap and flatten this in the same way.

6 Fold the top face of both flaps to the center and make creases.

7 Open up the left flap, flatten, and crease.

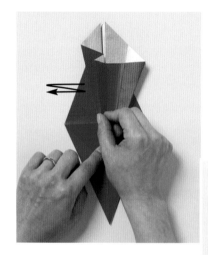

8 Turn the flap you have just folded back to the left along the center line and make a pleat fold. Open the unfolded right side and repeat the crease and pleat fold.

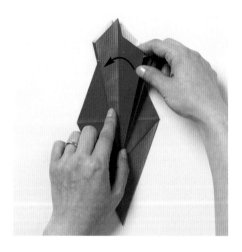

9 Open the flaps as in the photo and count out an even number of creases on each side.

10 Fold the triangle in the middle up.

11 Fold the paper in half lengthwise and make a crease.

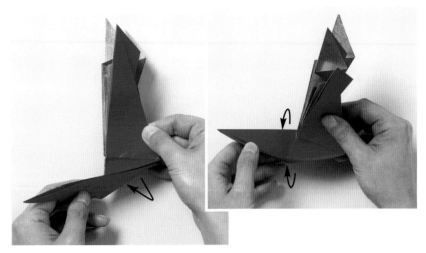

12 Unfold the object and while holding the fantail piece with the right hand, fold the left part back along the crease you made in step 10 to make a valley fold.

13 Make a crease at the middle of the left part. Unfold it and make an inside fold to form the bird's neck.

14 Make an inside fold at the tip to make the crane's head. Spread the wings and arrange the form of the crane.

75

USAGI—RABBIT

The image of a white rabbit is a favorite in Japan and frequently appears in ancient Japanese tales and folklore. One of the most traditional images in Japan is a rabbit on the moon, pounding rice cakes with a pestle and mortar. Here, I made a white rabbit with white paper, reminiscent of the folklore. It may seem difficult to fold at first, but after a little practice, you will make it with no trouble. Use different sizes of paper to make a rabbit family. Alternatively, you can use sheets of patterned paper to make a colorful grouping.

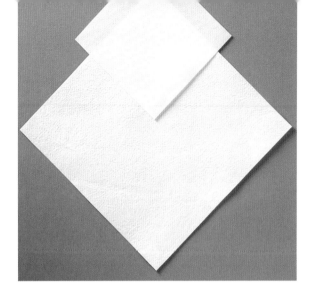

MATERIALS

◆ **2 sheets of plain paper, 12 x 12 in. (30 x 30cm) and 6 x 6 in. (15 x 15cm)**

◆ **Scissors**

Difficulty level: 5

1 Begin with the square fold (see page 16), taking care to make your creases accurate.

2 Fold the front right and left flaps to the center. Fold the bottom triangle up and make three creases.

3 Unfold into the square. Raise and open the front flap, pulling it down before flattening it.

4 Repeat these steps on the reverse side to leave the object in a long diamond shape.

5 Fold only the solid top flap from right to left to cover the two long arms. Then, fold the upper flap over to make a long, thin triangle.

6 Fold the top arm of the three piled flaps at right angles to the object about ⅜ in. (1 cm) from the center. Turn over and also fold up the bottom flap.

7 Pick the object up and, after turning it over, fold the center flap along the crease already made for the top and bottom flaps to make a marker crease. Open out the object and refold it back on itself so that the top and bottom flaps are now enclosed.

8 Pull down two-thirds of the enclosing flap that you just made in step 7. Then, make an inside fold half way up the flap you just pulled out, to make the rabbit's nose.

9 Open out the object and cut along the center line to the crease in the middle. Be careful not to cut the bottom sheet.

10 Take the top flap you just cut and bring it the left, folding it under itself to make a mountain fold.

11 Again, fold the same flap under itself in the middle. Crease the tip of the foot and fold inside. Repeat these steps on the other side.

12 Make a pleat fold for the tail. Unfold and turn it inside along the first crease, pulling out the tip at the second crease. Arrange the form.

SAKURA ZARA—
PLATE OF CHERRY BLOSSOM

The sakura, or cherry, is a special tree that has charmed the Japanese since ancient times. In spring, the cherry trees blossom throughout the country, covering the land with flower petals. I made this lovely plate by combining five petals folded from separate sheets of paper into the shape. Different patterns of paper would produce an entirely different effect. If you make the dish with rich, gorgeous paper, it can be used at a party, while a plate made from chic plain papcr would be perfect as a small container in the bedroom.

MATERIALS
◆ **5 sheets of colored paper, 6 x 6 in. (15 x 15cm)**
◆ **Glue**
◆ **Cocktail stick**

Difficulty level: 3

1 Fold the paper in half to make a horizontal crease in the middle of the paper. Unfold and fold the left and right sides into the center to make creases.

2 Fold the top corner down, using the folded flaps as the crease mark, to form a triangle.

3 Open the flaps out, folding the far end inside, then turn both sides over so that what were the short ends of the flaps meet together along the center line.

4 Halve the object by folding the right-hand side back underneath to the reverse side.

5 Fold the bottom triangle of paper away from you, making a crease along the edge of the flap.

6 Open out the top flap and fold the bottom edge up, inserting it into the upper triangle.

7 Fold back the flap you just opened in step 6, then use its far edge as the crease line to turn over the exposed triangle.

9 To open out the petal, start by flattening out the triangular part of the object.

8 Push the top triangle through the middle to make an inside fold. Make a crease at the bottom as shown in the photo.

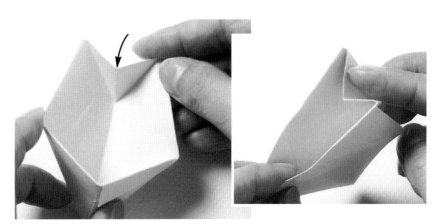

10 Carefully open out the object to form the final shape of the petal.

11 Make four more petals. Using a toothpick, place glue around their pointed ends and fit them together to make the plate.

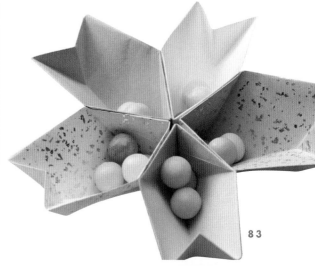

MARU UTSUWA—DISH

This design for an open container is possible by first making accurate creases, and then forming the paper into a multi-dimensional shape that's similar to the one you made for the cake box (see pages 40–43). The essential tip is to make neat and accurate creases. With different designs and sizes of paper, you can make dishes with different qualities, depending upon how you intend to use them. Your guests might find it difficult to believe that they are made from only a single piece of paper.

MATERIALS

◆ **1 sheet of patterned paper,
   12 x 12 in. (30 x 30cm)**

Difficulty level: 4

1 Begin with the paper's plain side upward. First make cross-shaped creases, then add quarter creases to all four squares. Unfold.

2 Fold in half to make a rectangle and fold the top flap forward on the diagonal to make a valley fold. Turn over and repeat on the other side. Unfold and fold in half the other way, and repeat making diagonal creases on both sides.

3 Unfold and place the paper face up. Pinch the quarter crease to make a mountain fold.

4 Carefully fold along the outer part of the diagonal crease to make a valley fold.

5 Hold each of these flaps together and fold them outward.

6 Repeat folding along the creases for all four sides to shape the paper into three dimensions.

7 Tuck the flaps you have lifted behind the folds to form the shape of the dish.

KODOMO BOSHI—CHILD'S HAT

One of the fun things about paper folding is creating new pieces from old or used papers. Here, a sheet of paper has been used to make a child's hat. Of course, it is also fun to make a balloon (see page 34) or a samurai helmet (see page 38), but this child's hat is quite simple to make and can be used as a party hat for adults as well as for children. It is preferable to use thin but strong and untearable paper, though you could also make it with old newspaper or gift wrap.

MATERIALS

◆ 1 sheet of plain paper, 12 x 12 in. (30 x 30cm) for a small hat, 21½ x 21½ in. (55 x 55 cm) for a medium hat, and 26 x 26 in. (65 x 65cm) for a large hat

Difficulty level: 1

1 Fold the paper in half to make a triangle then bring the right corner across to the other side of the object making a horizontal edge.

2 Take the left corner across to match.

3 Fold the front flap down in four equal sections to make creases.

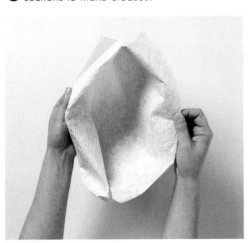

4 Fold the front flap down from the top along the creases one by one then turn over and repeat.

5 Holding in the edges gently ease the hat open.

6 Press the top in to create the final shape of the hat.

KASHI ZARA—TEA PLATE

There are many varieties of tea plates made from many different materials, including porcelain, earthenware, wood, and lacquer, to name but a few. Here, I have made a tea plate with modern, patterned paper. It is ideal for serving Japan's traditional dry candy, higashi, but you could treat your guests to chocolate or cookies if you prefer. Why not make it as a centerpiece for a tea party or a children's party; you'll be sure to create a talking point too.

MATERIALS

◆ **1 sheet of patterned paper, 6 x 6 in. (15 x 15cm)**

Difficulty level: 2

1 Begin with the triangle fold (see page 17) and then fold the corners of the front flap up to the top to make triangle creases.

2 Open up the lefthand triangle to make a square and repeat on the opposite side.

3 Fold both the right and left flaps of the square toward each other at the center of the square to make creases. Raise, open and flatten the left hand flap to make a petal in a long bamboo-leaf shape.

4 Repeat the previous step on the opposite side.

5 Place the petal along the center line, making a pleat fold underneath.

6 Turn the corners up toward the center and make square folds on both sides.

7 Use the same method as in steps 3 and 4 to make the outer petals.

AJISAI KAKEJIKU—
TAPESTRY WITH HYDRANGEA

First prepare the tapestry base from thick paper. Leave a space of about ½–¾ in. (1.5–2cm) at the top and bottom of the paper for the glue to attach it to a wooden dowel or bamboo as a tapestry rod so that you could roll it up. Here, I have decorated the tapestry with hydrangea flowers, or ajisai. You can apply any origami model in the place of the hydrangea used here—try making your own unique tapestry.

MATERIALS

- ◆ **1 piece of thin tabloid size (A3) cardstock**
- ◆ **Small flowers: 1 piece of paper, 6 x 6 in. (15 x 15cm), cut into 30 1 x 1 in. (2.5 x 2.5cm) squares**
- ◆ **Large flowers: 1 piece of paper, 6 x 6 in. (15 x 15cm), cut into 10 1¼ x 1¼ in. (3 x 3cm) squares**

- ◆ **Leaves: 2 pieces of plain paper 3½ x 3½ in. (8.5 x 8.5cm)**
- ◆ **Glue**
- ◆ **Cocktail stick**

Difficulty level: 3

MAKING THE FLOWERS

1 Place the white side of the paper face up and make a diagonal crease. Unfold and score, then repeat for the opposite corners. Fold the sheet in half twice, creating a square.

2 Squeeze the paper together into a cross shape and flatten onto the table. It is easier to make a square fold this way with a small piece of paper.

3 Fold the front flaps to the center. Repeat for the reverse side.

4 Fold the bottom corner up to the top point and make a score fold.

5 Holding the long point, pull the ends apart to open the top flaps, flattening the flower. Make 30 of them.

MAKING THE LEAVES

1 Fold the paper in half to make a triangle. Unfold and fold the top and bottom corners to the center. Fold the left corners to the center.

2 Fold the right tip downward and score—the angle of this fold determines the shape of the leaf.

3 Turn the point back on itself so that it lies along the center of the leaf.

4 Fold in half along the center line to make a valley fold.

5 Rotate the paper 180 degrees and fold the left tip ¼ in. (5mm) from the edge at an angle of 20 degrees and continue making pleat folds along the length of the leaf.

6 Unfold the pleats and open the object out into the leaf shape created earlier.

7 Paste the leaves and flowers onto the tapestry. Balance the whole picture; take care not to put too many flowers on top of each other.

SUPPLIERS

Special thanks to all the suppliers who kindly supplied materials for this book. The author unreservedly recommends them.

SUGIHARA WASHIPAPER INC.
17-2, Oizu, Echizen-shi,
Fukui 915-0235
Japan
Phone: +81-778-42-0032
Fax: +81-778-42-0144
e-mail: sugihara@washiya.com
www.washiya.com/index1.html (Japanese)
www.washiya.com/english.htm (English)

KARACHO STUDIO
e-mail: mailto@karacho.co.jp
www.karacho.co.jp (Japanese)

AWAGAMI FACTORY
136 Kawahigashi, Yamakawa-cho,
Yoshinogawa-shi,
Tokushima 779-3401
Japan
Tel: +81-883-42-2772
e-mail: info@awagami.or.jp
www.awagami.jp (Japanese)
www.awagami.com (English)

INTERNATIONAL ORIGAMI CENTER
Yushimano Kobayashi Corporation
(Origami Kaikan), 1-7-14 Yushima, Bunkyo-ku,
Tokyo 113-0034
Japan
Tel: +81-3-3811-4025
Fax: +81-3-3815-3348
e-mail: admin@origamikaikan.co.jp
www.origamikaikan.co.jp (Japanese)
www.origamikaikan.co.jp/lp/english_guide.
html (English)

WAGAMI-DO
3-5-15, Izumi-cho, Sakado-shi,
Saitama 350-0231
Japan
Tel: +81-49-277-5590
Fax: +81-49-277-5590
e-mail: info@wagamido.jp
www.wagamido.jp (Japanese)
www.wagamido.com (English)

ONAO LTD.
184-3 Takata Taisho,
Ichikawadaimon-cho,
Nishiyatsushiro-gun,
Yamanashi 409-3606
Japan
Tel: +81-55-272-0321
Fax: +81-55-272-0323
e-mail: info@onao.co.jp
www.onao.co.jp (Japanese and English)

KAMIYAKATA SHIMAYU LTD.
2-4-25 Ote, Matsumoto-shi,
Nagano 390-0874
Japan
Tel: +81-263-35-1000
Fax: +81-263-36-6554
e-mail: info@shimayu.co.jp
www.shimayu.co.jp (Japanese)

USEFUL BOOKS AND WEBSITES

Special thanks to the origami artists and creators who consented to their inclusion in this book (see page 96).

BOOKS
Fun with Origami by Kazuo Kobayashi (Kodansha International Ltd.)
Origami Zakka Book by Kazuo Kobayashi (Bunka Publishing Bureau)
Kantan Origami 100 by Kazuo Kobayashi (Nihon Vogue-Sha Co. Ltd.)
Origami Zakka— 12 Months of Origami Sundries by Rika Masahisa
(Kawade Shobo Shinsha Publishers)
The Encyclopedia of Origami Techniques by Nick Robinson
(Search Press Ltd.)

JAPANESE-LANGUAGE WEBSITES
Round R, Rika Masahisa: roundr.moon.bindcloud.jp
Origami Club: www.origami-club.com
Explantae: explantae.theshop.jp

ENGLISH-LANGUAGE WEBSITES
Japan Origami Academic Society: www.origami.jp/en/
Nippon Origami Association: www.origami-noa.jp
British Origami Society: www.britishorigami.org
Origami Club: www.en.origami-club.com

MATERIALS DIRECTORY
If you have difficulty purchasing any of the Japanese papers used in
this book, cannot contact the information sources mentioned above, or
have any queries, please do not hesitate to get in contact with me at the
following site, where I will be very happy to assist:
www.mari-ono.com/contact

INDEX

ACKNOWLEDGMENTS

No book is written alone. This achievement represents the sum of the generous help and co-operation given by family, friends, and many others. My special thanks go to Yukiko Tagawa for translating my draft; to Chizuko Tokuno, Natsuko Watanabe and Mr. Tsutomu Nakai for much useful advice; to Michael Herbstler for proofreading; to Mr. and Mrs. Hancock and their son, Thomas; and to the Deerhurst & Apperley C of E School, and the staff of the National Trust shop at Polesden Lacey in Surrey for their sincere cooperation. Thanks also to Georgina Harris, Cindy Richards, and Robin Gurdon for editing; to Geoff Dann for taking photos; to Christine Wood for designing this book; to Masaharu and Yoko Ono, my parents at home in Japan for their continued support; and finally to my son Roshin, for acting as the model for the child's hat and for all his other support. I also thank all those who were involved in publishing this book, and all the readers of this book for being interested in Japanese papercrafts and Japanese traditional culture.

My biggest thanks go, as usual, to my husband Takumasa for his continued encouragement, always useful suggestions, comments, and help.

ORIGAMI DESIGN CREDITS
Special thanks to the origami artists and creators who consented to the inclusion of their original designs in this book:

Page 30 Based on a unit by Mitsononbu Sonobe / Pages 62, 90,94,114 Rika Masahisa /Page 100 Toshio Chino / Page 108 Mitsue Nakano /Page 112 Nick Robinson.

Design of Japanese papers:
Reproduced by permission of IKIYA in Japan
http://www.ikiya.jp/